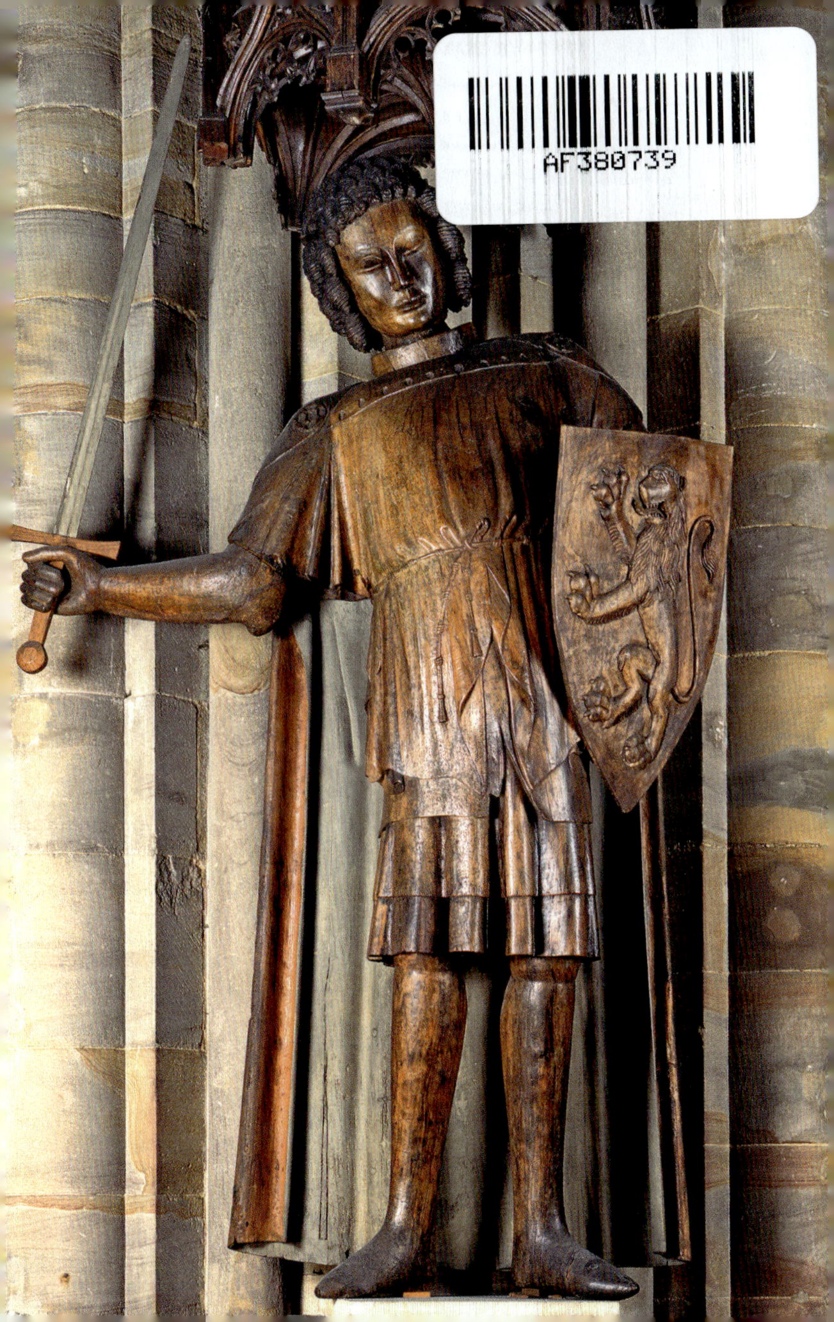
AF380739

Major municipal events were also celebrated in St. Reinold's church, the most important of which, given how much was written about it, was Emperor Charles IV's visit to Dortmund in November 1377: as the secular ruler of the city, the Emperor was received with a procession in front of the city gates, in which the precious reliquary (now lost but born witness to in a description of the 18th century) with the relics of Reinold were carried. The procession led him through the eastern gate and via the Hellweg directly into St. Reinold's church for prayer. On the following day the mayors (they alone had power of the keys) opened the shrine to gift some relics of the patron saint to the Emperor, which to this day rest in St. Vitus' Cathedral in Prague.

For many believers in the Middle Ages, the relics of Reinold were also a destination for pilgrimage. This changed after the Reformation of the church from 1562/1570 on. St. Reinold's became protestant, the worship of the patron saint declined in city life. The relics were taken to Cologne at the beginning of the 17th century by families of the council who had remained Catholics and from there, via Brussels, the relics finally arrived in Toledo, Spain, where they are still part of the reliquary treasury. During the celebration of Dortmund's 1100th anniversary in 1982, the relics were brought back to the city for a short time. They were divided up, and since then the provost church has enshrined a relic of the patron saint in a golden reliquary on the main altar – Reinold has returned to his city.

Before the Reformation, St. Reinold's was the seat of an archdeacon who was responsible for a large area between the rivers Lippe and Ruhr, between Oberhausen and Hamm. Numerous churches in the region were placed under the mother church of St. Reinold. All this changed with the Reformation and changed to an even greater extent with the Enlightenment and Secularisation in the time of the French Revolution: faith and world, religion and state were strictly separated – city politics abandoned the church, St. Reinold's was no longer one of the main centres of the city. Since the early 18th century St. Reinold's functions were limited to being the most important place of worship for Protestants in the city, a development which was strengthened by industrialisation from 1850.

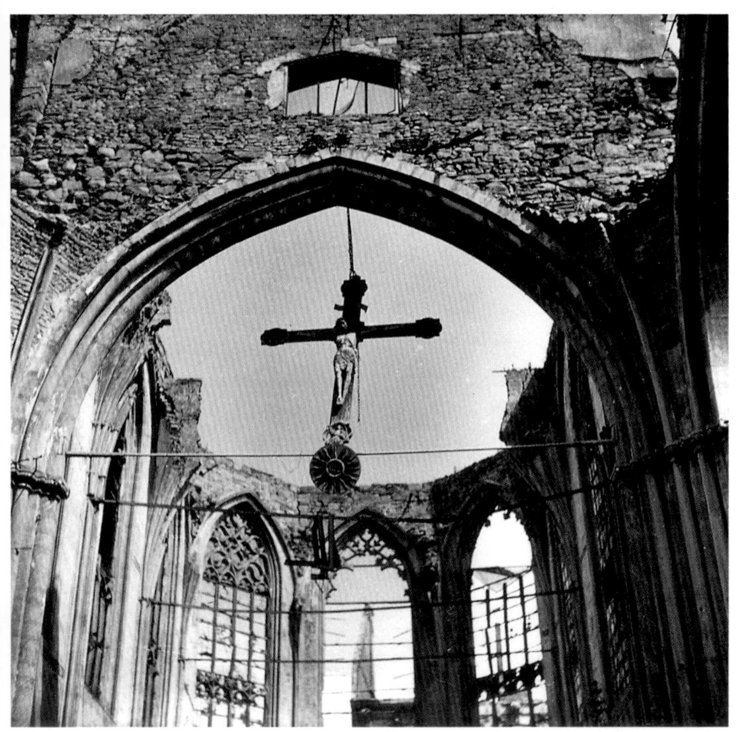

▲ *St. Reinold's after the destruction, photographed by Erich Angenendt, 1946*

At the turn of the 20th century, in a historicization phase of public awareness, the intense perception of the "glorious history" of the city in the Middle Ages began. Dortmund was now remembered as the prosperous imperial city and Hanseatic town of the late Middle Ages and the view of St. Reinold as a patron saint, a "unique feature" of the city returned to the forefront of public perception.

After the National Socialist dictatorship and the devastation of the Second World War, one of the first goals of the inhabitants of the city was to reconstruct St. Reinold's as far as possible in its original form –the church and church institutions offered direct help in every day life, but above all they offered spiritual guidance and identity which provided a link to the time before 1933. In the post-war period, in the thoughts and actions of the people, St. Reinold's was the landmark of the city, a symbol of new beginning. The reconstruction of St. Reinold's, which took place while people in the city which was almost completely destroyed suffered from a shortage of food and accommodation, happened through great support from many people: through donations, contributions and a large raffle. In 1956 the reconstruction, which was entrusted to the architect Herwarth Schulte, was completed: Dortmund's landmark was restored.

In 2006, the *Reinoldiforum* was built on the floor plan of the chapel to the southwest of St. Reinold's, which was built after the First World

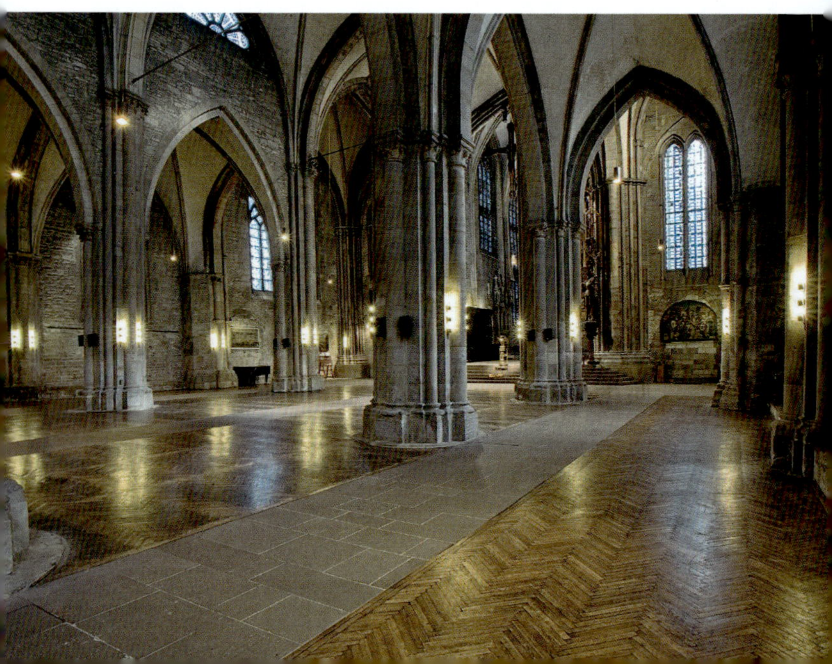

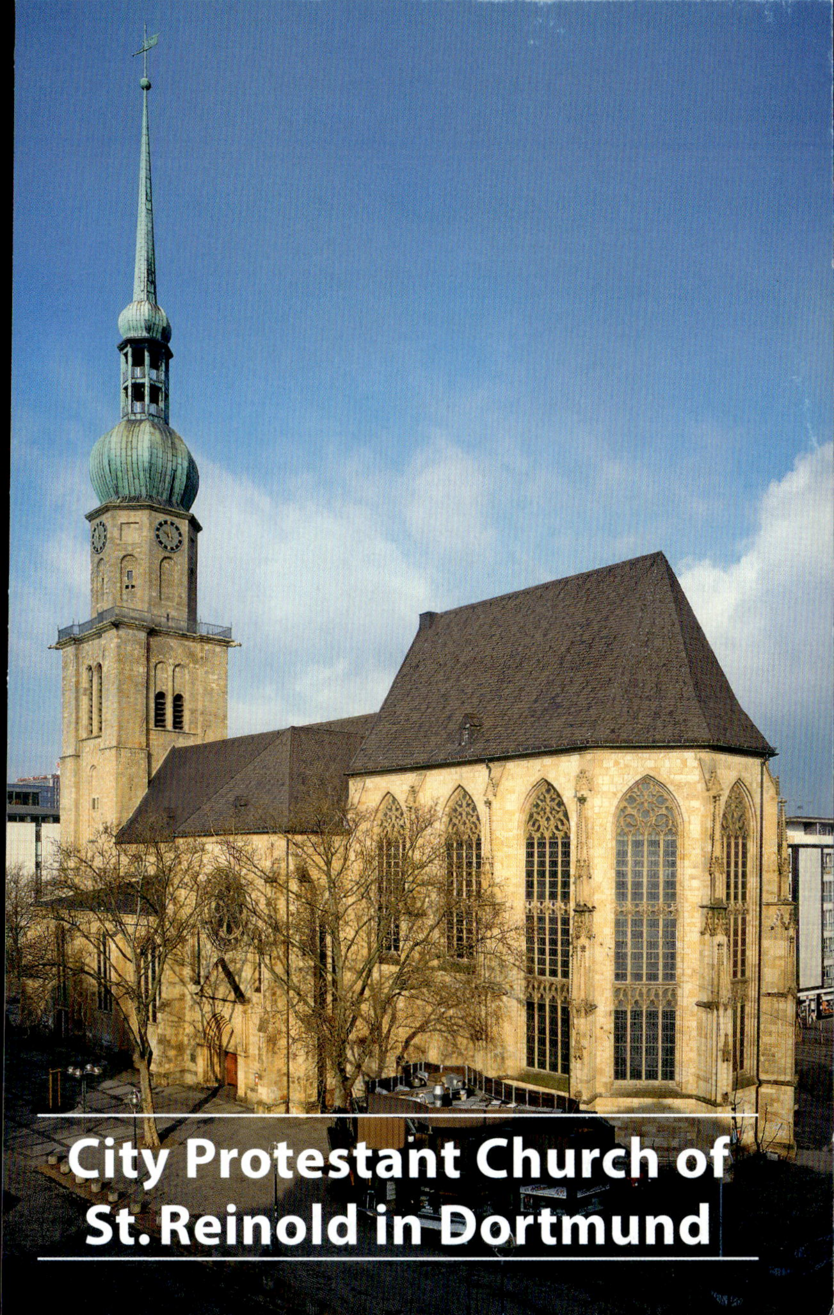
City Protestant Church of
St. Reinold in Dortmund

City Protestant Church of St. Reinold in Dortmund

by Thomas Schilp and Barbara Welzel

St. Reinold's – a changing city church

St. Reinold's church has a long tradition. However, its roots are concealed in darkness and only a few details of its history can be made out. It is likely that an earlier church had stood here long before Dortmund developed to a city in the 12th and early 13th century. After the subjugation of Saxony by the Franks led by Charlemagne, initially, around the year 800, a royal castle with a settlement was erected at the crossing of the Hellweg, with a trunk road from Cologne via Dortmund to the north. For Ottonian kings in the 10th century, this place was an important link between the power base of the royal dynasty in the Harz area and the imperial centre in the west: Dortmund was built up from a stronghold of the kingdom to an important royal palace. From then on, while on their travels the ruling kings held their imperial assemblies and court parliaments in Dortmund and also celebrated Easter here on many occasions. The palaces had to be able to satisfy the representative requirements of royalty. As well as the King's accommodation and provision, along with his cortege and the challenges of receiving numerous high-ranking guests, another task was the palace church, which we can safely assume stood on the site of today's St. Reinold's church. Archaeological excavations have in any case confirmed evidence of an earlier 10th century church corresponding to the church that stands today.

What is unknown is when the relics of the patron saint of Dortmund, St. Reinold, were transferred from Cologne to Dortmund. We can only assume that this could have happened with the construction of the royal palace in the 10th century or in the period of a radical church reform (in the context of the so-called Investiture Controversy) in the second half of the 11th century under Archbishop Anno II of Cologne. Indicative of the second assumption is that later Dort-

View of chancel to the east ▶

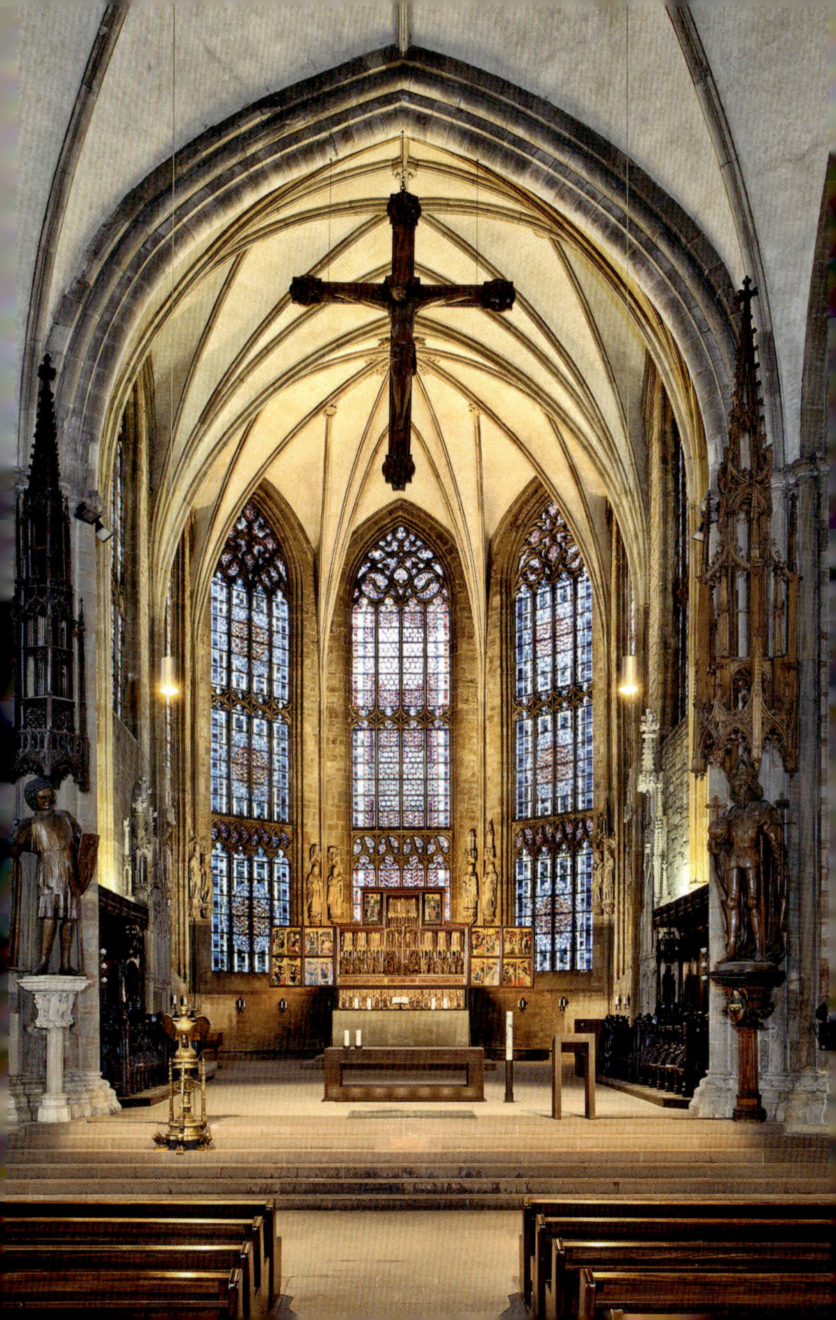

mund records repeatedly report of a change of the patron saint of the church from St. Pantaleon's to St. Reinold's in this period.

St. Reinold's burned down in a large fire that engulfed the city in 1231/1232; after the destruction, work soon began on a new building: a basilica with three naves, which we can still admire today in the forms of the nave. The imposing high chancel emerged between 1421 and 1450 as a magnificent expansion of the chancel of the 13th century and can be attributed to the master builder Roseer.

St. Reinold, the patron of the church, was the patron of the municipality. In the Middle Ages, without the relics of the patron saint, the imperial city and the Hanseatic town was unthinkable: Reinold was a sacral focus which bound the municipality together, he offered citizens and inhabitants protection; he functioned as a battle aid and according to medieval representation, he was actively involved in the daily life of bustling Dortmund; he gave Dortmund its identity – and to this day St. Reinold and St. Reinold's church are still of particular importance to Dortmund. The medieval merchants took their patron saint with them on trading trips, as can be seen from the worship of the patron saint of Dortmund in towns in the Baltic Sea region, such as in Gdansk or Toruń. The relics of this patron were located almost entirely in Dortmund; the city had its patron saint almost completely to itself. As well as the town hall and market place, the St. Reinold's church was one the central public places and an important assembly point in the city. As representative of the municipality, the council took its permanent place in the high chancel to the north, in the council seats in front of the chamber of sacred relics, in which the bones of the patron saint rested; the clerics of the church and the city sat to the south, in front of the second chamber of sacred relics (the resting place for other relics, no longer known today). The original sacrament house no longer remains. The chancel served as the chapel for the council; it was used for council church services after the annual council election in February and it was used for representative purposes. Here, in front of the relics and next to the larger than life sculpture of St. Reinold, legal acts were certified and important trade agreements were concluded in the Middle Ages.

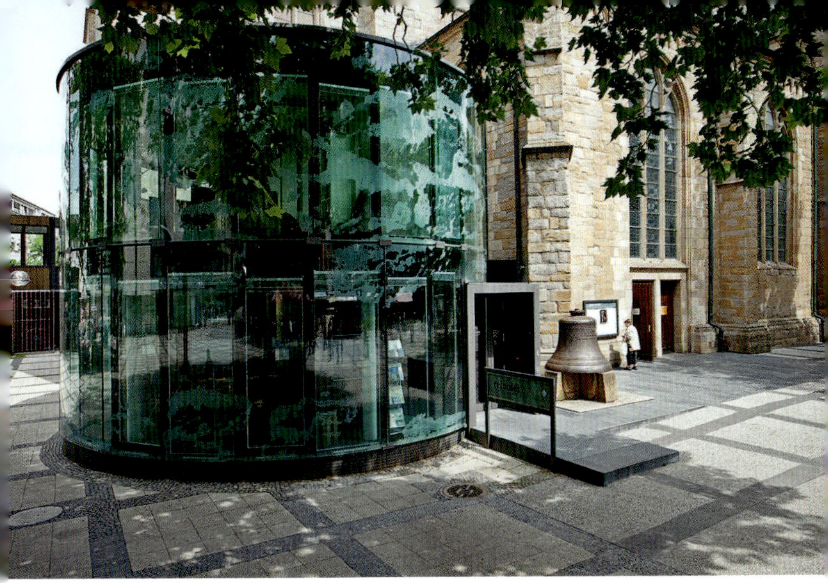

▲ *Exterior view with the Reinoldiforum*

War and destroyed during the Second World War. It was constructed according to the plans of the "architecten schröder schulte-ladbeck". This transparent construction is the Protestant church's reaction to structural changes in church and in society. The opening of the city church to the community of Dortmund refers to the pre-modern tradition of the city's main church.

◀ *View of the nave from the side nave*

Saint Reinold

The legend of Saint Reinold is based in the time of Charlemagne during the Saxon wars. After the noble son of the powerful knight Haymon killed a son of Charlemagne in a fight, he fled with his brothers on Bayard, the magic horse. When, after numerous battles, Reinold had also lost his fortified castle of Montaubon, the hero fled to Dortmund where, as ruler of the city, he owned another castle. Finally a peace agreement was reached with Charlemagne here. The hero submitted and handed over his loyal steed Bayard to the ruler, only for the horse to escape. Reinold then went on a voyage of penance to the Holy Land where he conquered Jerusalem. On his return he devoted his life to religion, working on the construction of Cologne cathedral. He was killed out of envy and his body thrown into the Rheine. Miraculously, fish brought the body to the water's surface and he was recovered. The cart for bringing him back to the city drove to Dortmund by itself, where all bells began to chime and ill were cured. He was buried in his city and has been worshipped as patron saint of the city ever since.

Architecture and furnishings

To date St. Reinold's church, as well as Dortmund's high-rise buildings from the Dortmund "U" to the RWE tower, is an important landmark in the Dortmund skyline. The 13th century nave combines the evidently majestic design of the basilica with the high side naves of a hall church. This is how the fan-shaped, halved window roses developed. The chancel, which is set higher than the nave and transept, was built between 1421 and 1450; the older chancel was demolished to accommodate it. Its effect is dominated by the large windows, which are divided by four-track tracery. The windows in the end wall of the transept are also part of this building phase.

During this challenging construction stage of the 15th century, stained glass windows with complex iconography were created. In the apex, the representation of the Emperor with the seven electoral princes gives an account of the importance of the city. These windows were sadly lost in the Second World War.

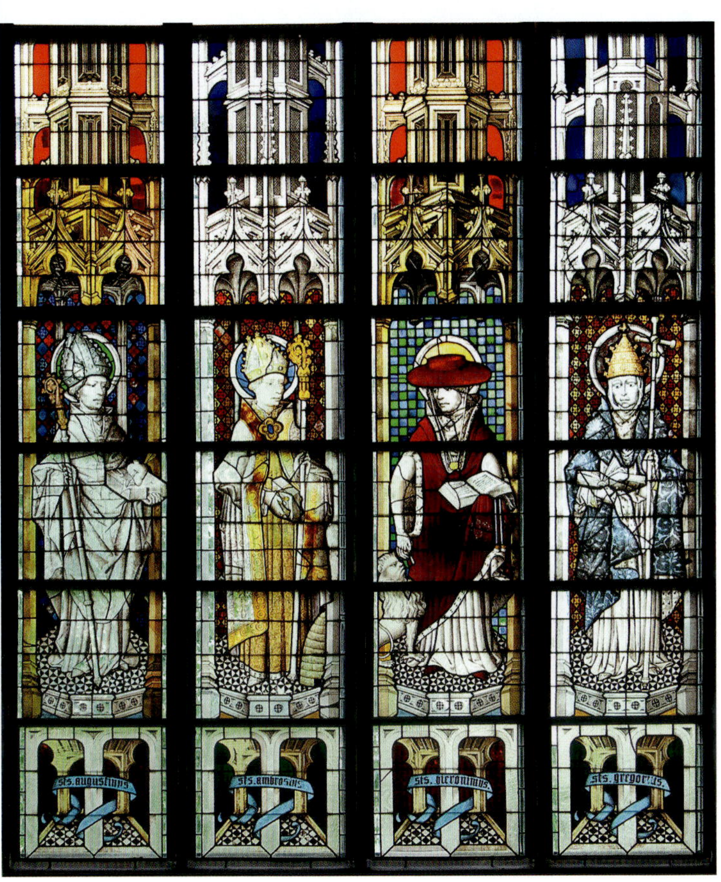

▲ *Church Fathers, stained glass chancel window from the middle of the 15th century, today in the tower*

Pages 12/13: *Winged altar, early 15th century*

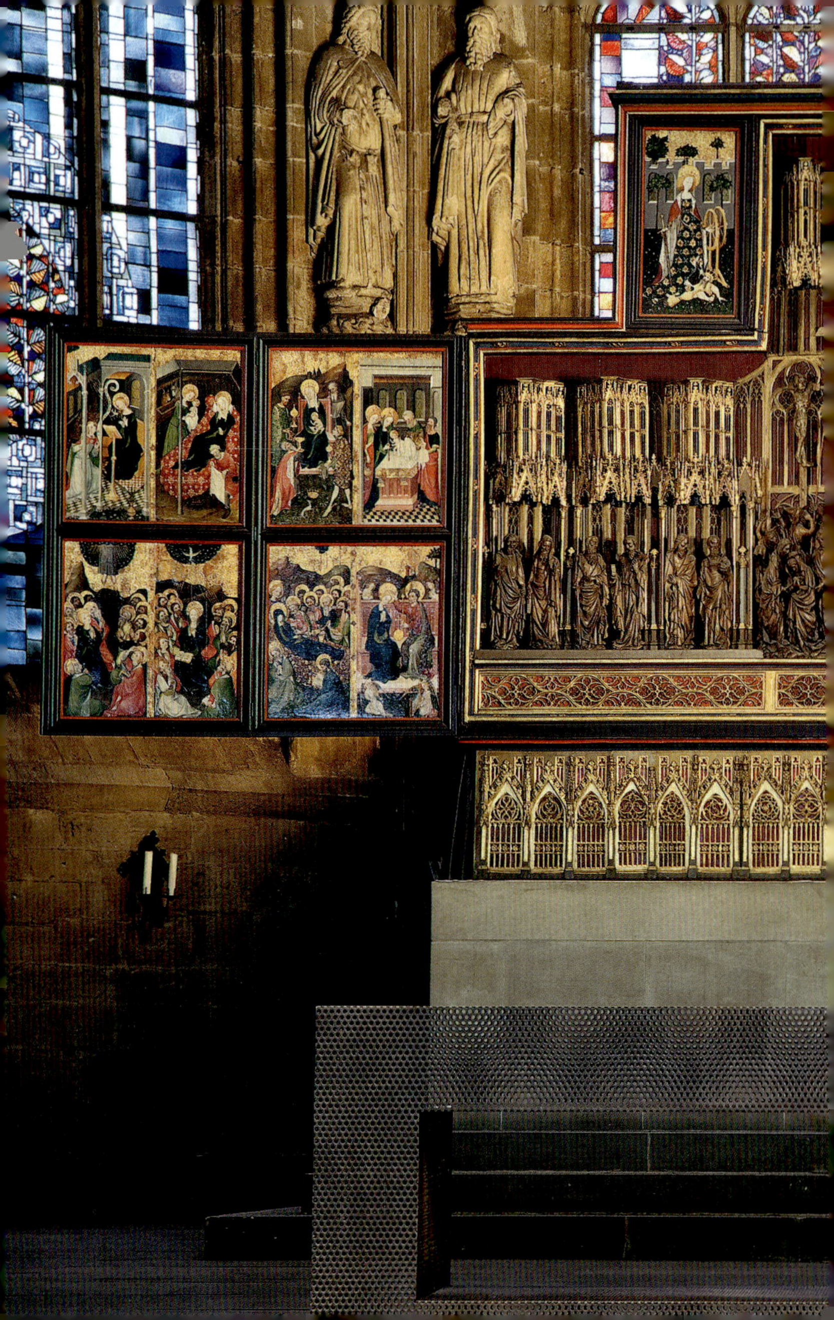

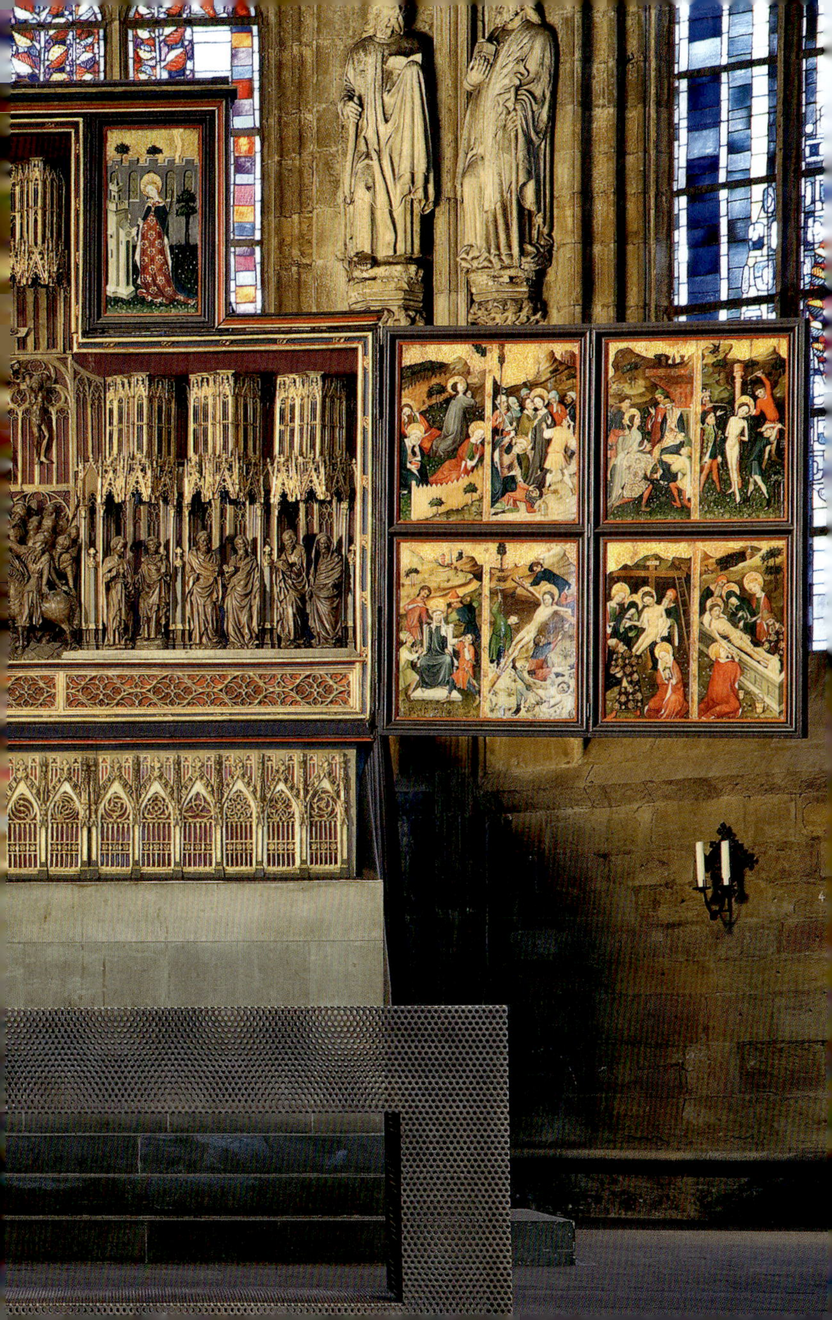

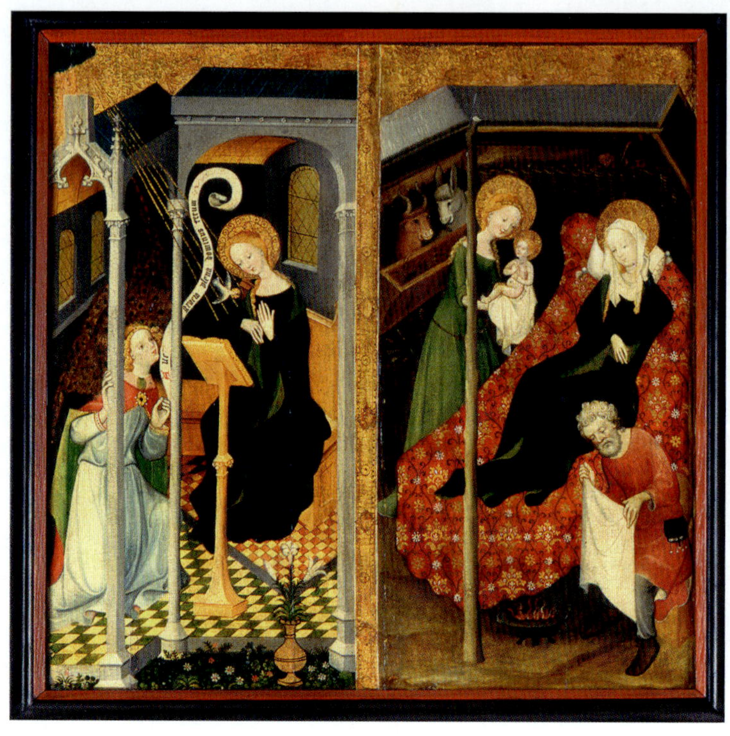

▲ *Annunciation and birth of Jesus, paintings on altar wings*

All that is left is an image with four Fathers of the Church, which has been moved to the tower. The reconstruction of the church after the Second World War did not revert back to old building methods and materials: today the church has an iron truss; the merging of old and new can be seen particularly in the tower. The reconstruction of the tower was uncertain for a long time. The ruin was more than once threatened with demolition, before, after a contest, the design based on the Baroque tower was decided upon and subsequently executed.

     Pair of apostles, group of figures from the shrine ▶

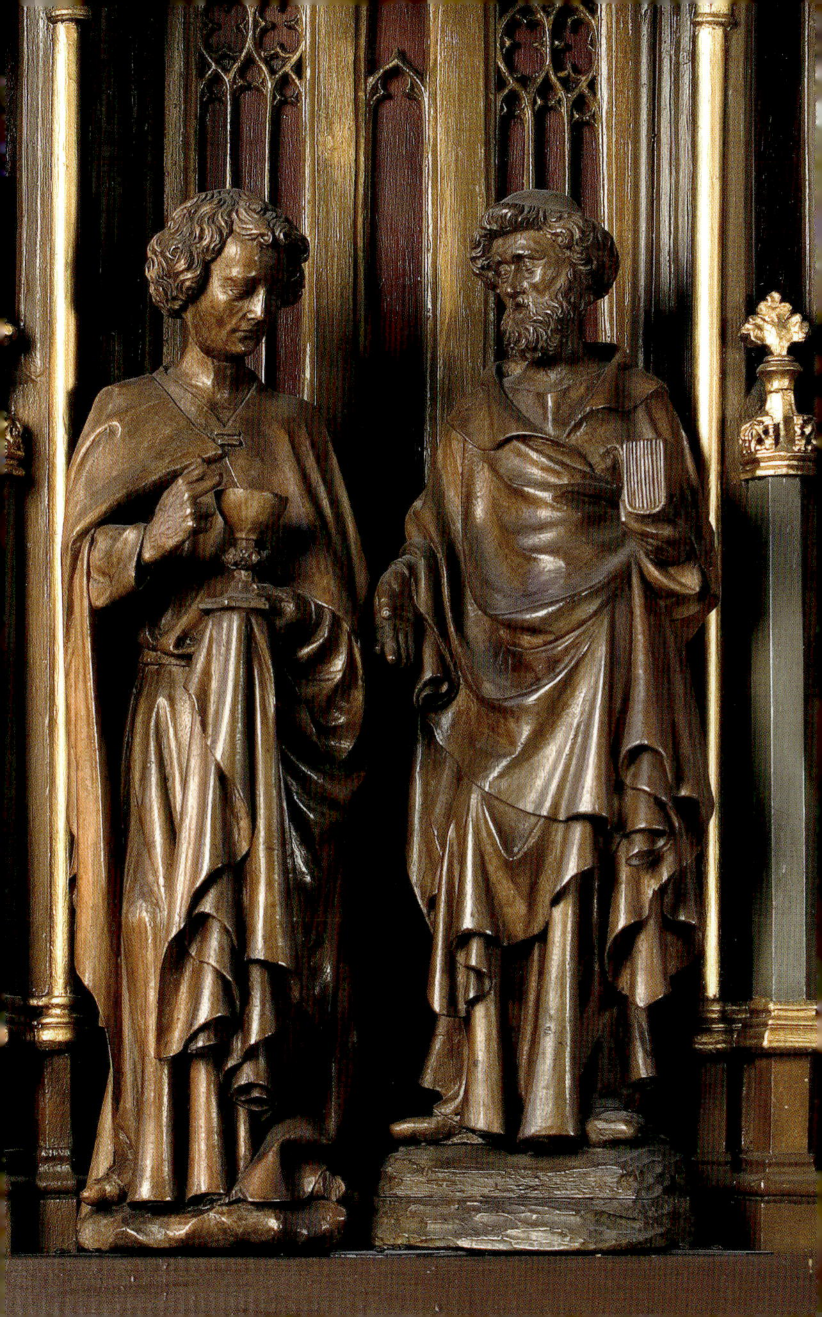

At its reopening the church had clear windows fitted as a provisional measure. Only in 1967/68 was the whole church fitted with stained glass windows made by Hans Gottfried von Stockhausen. He consciously abandoned figurative, narrative forms in his windows, and instead opted to restore the colour and light space of St. Reinold's using contemporary forms of expression. Technically however, Stockhausen reverted back to medieval art and used stained glass, which was joined with metal strips. Furthermore, he painted the individual panes elaborately by hand.

The new construction of the chancel adopted two significant decorative items from the earlier 13th century construction: the effigy of the patron saint and the altar retable. The larger-than-life **figure of Saint Reinold** dates from about 1300 and since the end of the 15th century it has been accompanied by Charlemagne, the legendary founder of the city, at the opposite chancel pillar. Reinold, heavenly patron of the city, as is written in medieval sources, is shown as protective hero, with the ability to defend his city. Only through scientific reconstruction of the coloured paint on the figure (it was stripped after different changing layers of paint), can the the appearance of the figure be made out: the patron saint wore chain mail as well as the chain stockings of a noble knight, and wore garments made of precious material both on top and underneath. In the years after 1300 such fabrics were imported from the Orient, even from China. They were very valuable and are a clear testimony to the wide reach of long-distance trade. The sculpture combines the different facets of the person and the legend of the patron saint: his background and the stage of his life as a knight on one side, and the renunciation of this sort of life on the other. In this regard, contrary to the clothing norms of the Middle Ages, the patron saint does not wear a noble belt over his tabard, but rather the simple, knotted rope. The pigments from which the colours for painting were made (and also the the altar paintings) were imported from all four corners of the world.

Mourning Mary, John and Longinus,
Group of figures from the shrine ▶

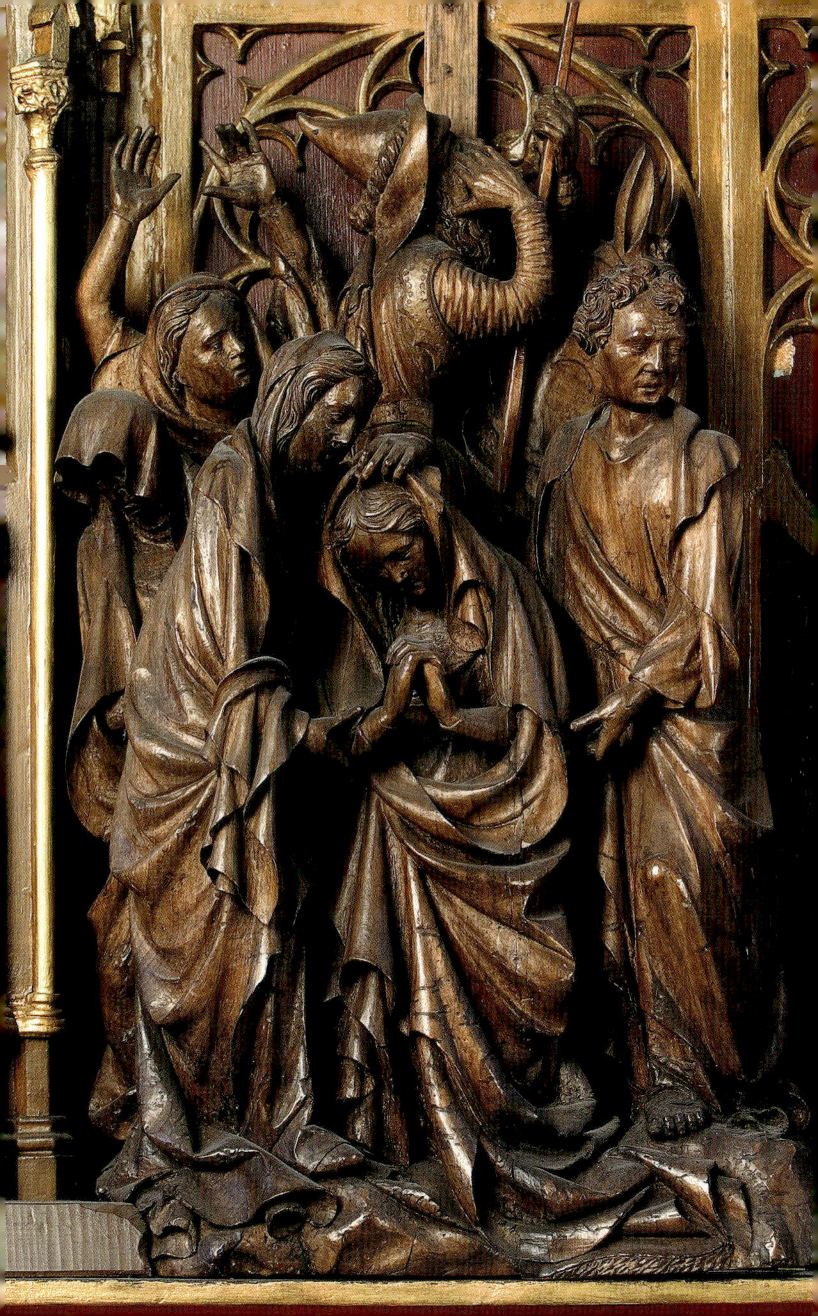

Where it stood the statue was accessible to all Dortmund inhabitants (except for lepers and Jews). In terms of such perception situations, one should fundamentally reconsider the distinction that is often made between high and everyday culture. In particular it must be said that the figure shaped the perceptions of all Dortmund inhabitants of their patron saint and facilitated the communication of such perceptions.

The **main altar** is adorned with an altar retable created around 1410/20 in the Netherlands. In the elevated centre, the sculptures of the shrine show the crucifixion with the Mother of God collapsing with grief on the right of Jesus and with the good captain on the left, the twelve apostles on both sides, in groups of two respectively set in the elaborate tracery architecture. These sculptures are among the highlights of Netherlandish sculpture from the beginning of the 15th century. You only have to visualise the fineness of the carvings: perhaps comparable with musical ornaments, the folds of the clothing, not one the same, encircling the figures axis to various depths, making the garments seem like virtuoso pieces. Furthermore, when one considers that clothing indeed represents the most important social code of the Middle Ages, it becomes clear how much focus was placed on the clothing of the sculptures. The paintings on the wings (eight scenes respectively) of the opened retable (the exterior sides are lost) are dedicated to the Passion and the life of the Virgin Mary with stages of Jesus' childhood. They represent the most extensive, surviving series of Netherlandish painting before Jan van Eyck. At the end of the 14th century the Duke of Burgundy ordered two Netherlandish altar works for his chapel near Dijon. They mark the beginning of an increasingly expanding export production of altar retables in Netherlandish cities until the first half of the 16th century. At the end of this development the "Golden Wonder" emerged as one of the highlights in the St. Petri church in Dortmund. The artistic quality of the sculptural decoration of the work in St. Reinold's matches that of the two ducal retables.

Eagle lectern, Netherlands, 15th century ▶

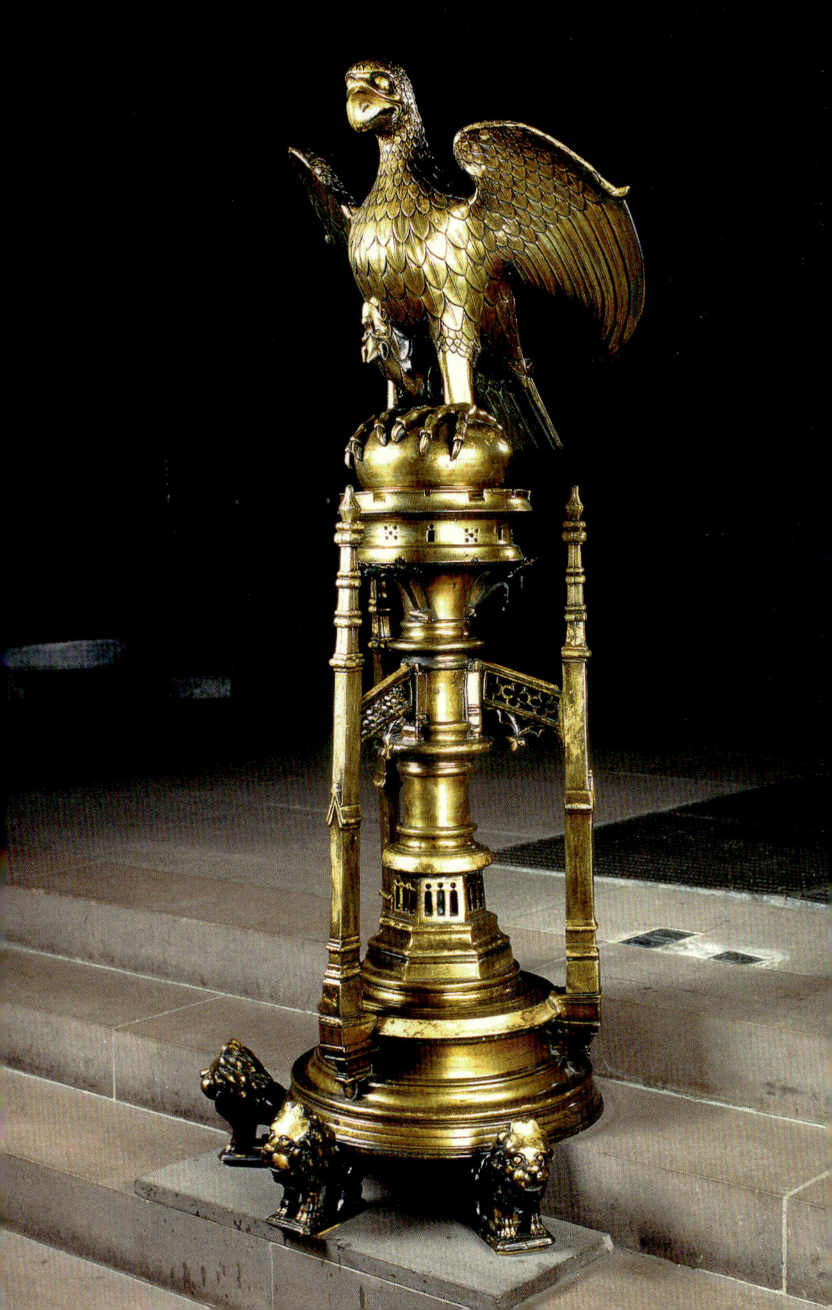

It probably came from Bruges to Dortmund. It is therefore testament to the far-reaching trade network of Dortmund trades people, who can be found in the ruling circles of the Hanseatic kontors in Bruges, and also to the cultural prestige that the long-distance trades people in Dortmund possessed.

The new chancel from the mid-15th century was fitted gradually. In 1462 the church had the choir stalls made for 42 people, commissioning the foreign carver Hermann Brabender, who probably came from Unna, for this work, which elaborately combines shrine and carving works and which in addition to figures on the side profiles, shows a whole cosmos of mythical creatures, scenes of a backwards world, etc on the seats.

The **baptistry** dating from 1469 which bears the marks of damage in the Second World War was cast by Johannes Winnenbrock, as is inscribed on the base. It is the last remaining work of the important Dortmund bell founder in St. Reinold's, and even in the whole of Dortmund city centre. This workshop was active over several generations and exported beyond the region. For example, the Maria bell in St. Patroclus' Church in Soest was made here. In 1473, Winnenbrock created the Reinold bell for the main city church of his home city. In 1897, this bell, together with all of the church bells, was melted down. In the first half of the 20th century St. Reinold's had chimes from steel bells, which in turn were lost in the Second World War. The badly damaged Emperor's bell was placed in front of the church as a memorial for peace. Today St. Reinold's has six cast steel bells, which were first sounded on Christmas Eve 1954. Tones: f° – b° – des1 – es1 – f1.

The **triumphal crucifix**, which dates from the second half of the 15th century, must be given a particular mention as a work which survived the decimation of the church's fittings after the introduction of the Reformation and then once again in the Second World War. As impressive photographs prove, the crucifix survived the war destruction in the triumphal arch.

Emperor's bell 1917/1918, placed in front of the church as a memorial after destruction in the Second World War ▶

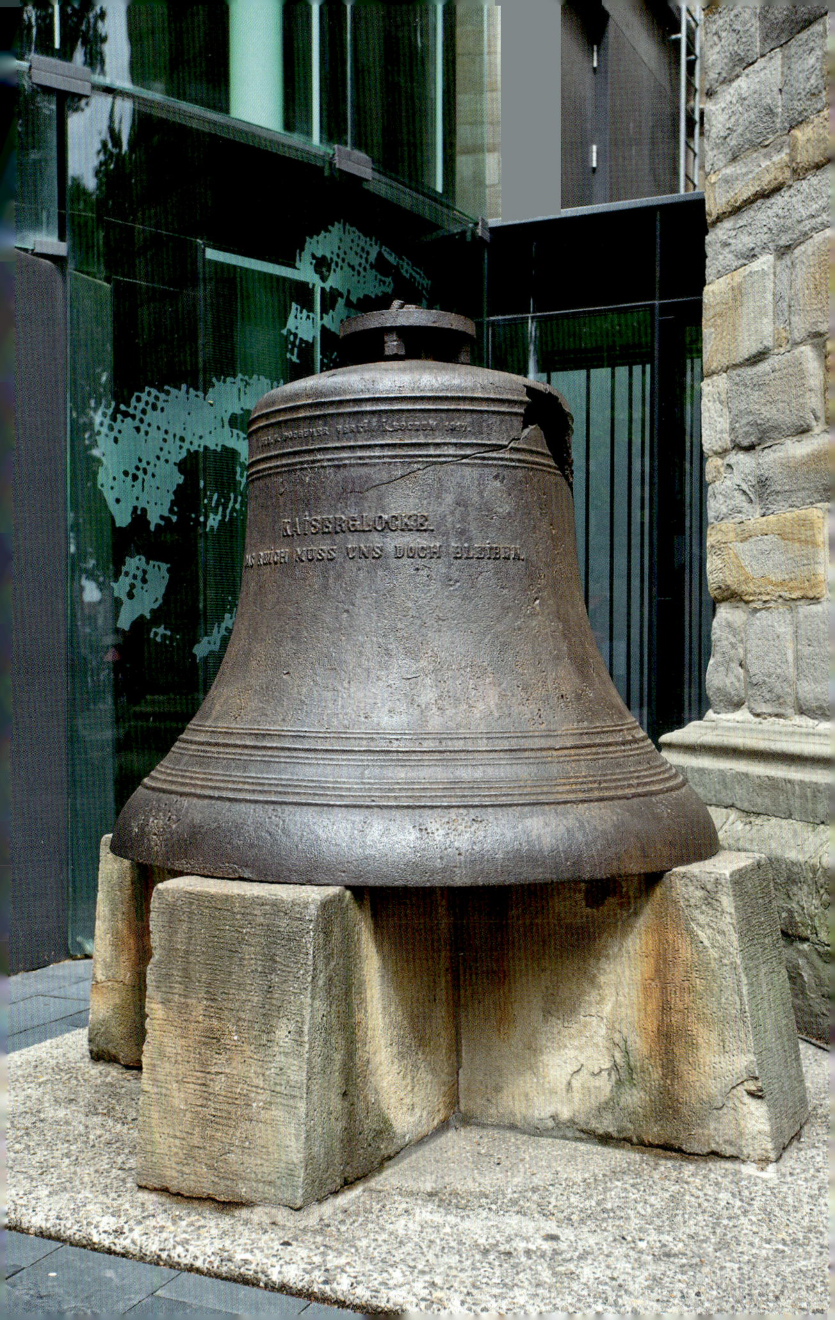

KAISERGLOCKE.
DAS REICH MUSS UNS DOCH BLEIBEN.

Stone figures of apostles have found a permanent home on the chancel pillars. The stone sculpture of the Virgin and Child above the door to the sacristy originates from the same period. In turn, the eagle lectern was imported from the Netherlands in the 15th century and is once again testament to the cultural interconnectedness of Dortmund.

In 1909 St. Reinold's obtained an **organ** from Walcker organ builders, which at that time, was one of the greatest romantic organs. Max Reger and Albert Schweizer, among others, came to Dortmund to play it. After its destruction in the Second World War, a newly built organ, again by Walcker, was inaugurated by Gerard Bunck in 1958. It is one of the biggest church organs in Westphalia and in line with prevailing post-war taste, the organ is orientated towards the neo-Baroque sound ideal.

In 2009 St. Reinold's obtained a **new altar** table as well as a second **pulpit**. Both bronze works were realised by Father Abraham in the forge of Königsmünster Abbey, according to the plans of architect Ulrich Wiegmann.

Selected Literature

Nils Büttner / Thomas Schilp / Barbara Welzel (Ed.), Städtische Repräsentation. St. Reinoldi und das Rathaus als Schauplätze des Dortmund Mittelalters (Dortmunder Mittelalter-Forschungen 5), Bielefeld 2005

Thomas Schilp / Barbara Welzel (Ed.), Stadtführer Dortmund im Mittelalter (Dortmunder Mittelalter-Forschungen 6), Bielefeld 2006

Matthias Ohm / Thomas Schilp / Barbara Welzel (Ed.), Ferne Welten – Freie Stadt. Dortmund im Mittelalter. Exhibition catalogue Dortmund 2006 (Dortmunder Mittelalter-Forschungen 7), Bielefeld 2006

Evelyn Bertram-Neunzig, Das Altarretabel in der Dortmunder St. Reinoldikirche (Dortmund Mittelalter-Forschungen 10), Bielefeld 2007

Eva Dietrich, Die westfälische Denkmalpflege der Nachkriegszeit (Denkmalpflege und Forschung in Westfalen 48), Münster 2008

Judith Zepp, St. Reinoldi in Dortmund, Dissertation TU Dortmund 2008, shortly going to print.

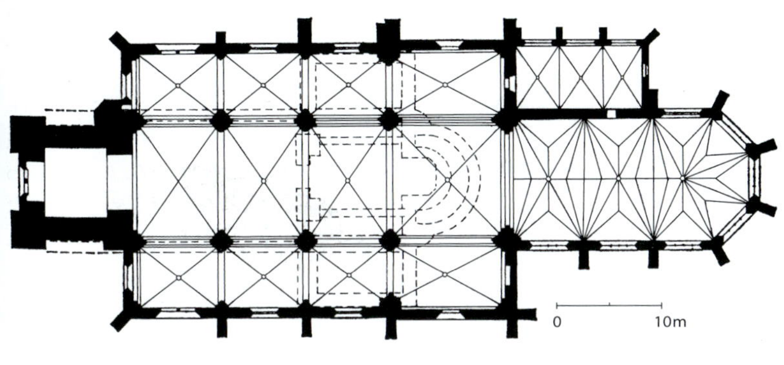

▲ *Floorplan*

City Protestant Church of St. Reinold in Dortmund

Stadtkirchenbüro St. Reinoldi-Kirche
Ostenhellweg 2
44135 Dortmund

Tel. +49 (0)231 / 882 30 13 · Fax +49 (0)231 / 882 30 16
www.sanktreinoldi.de

Published by the
City Protestant Church of St. Reinold, Michael Küstermann,
and the Protestant Parish of St. Reinold, Ulrich Dröge.

Photographs: Rüdiger Glahs / Diethelm Wulfert, Dortmund. –
Erich Angenendt, Dortmund City Archive Collection: page 8.
Printing: F&W Mediencenter, Kienberg

Front cover: Exterior view from the south-east
Back page: Baptistry, Johannes Winnenbrock, 1469

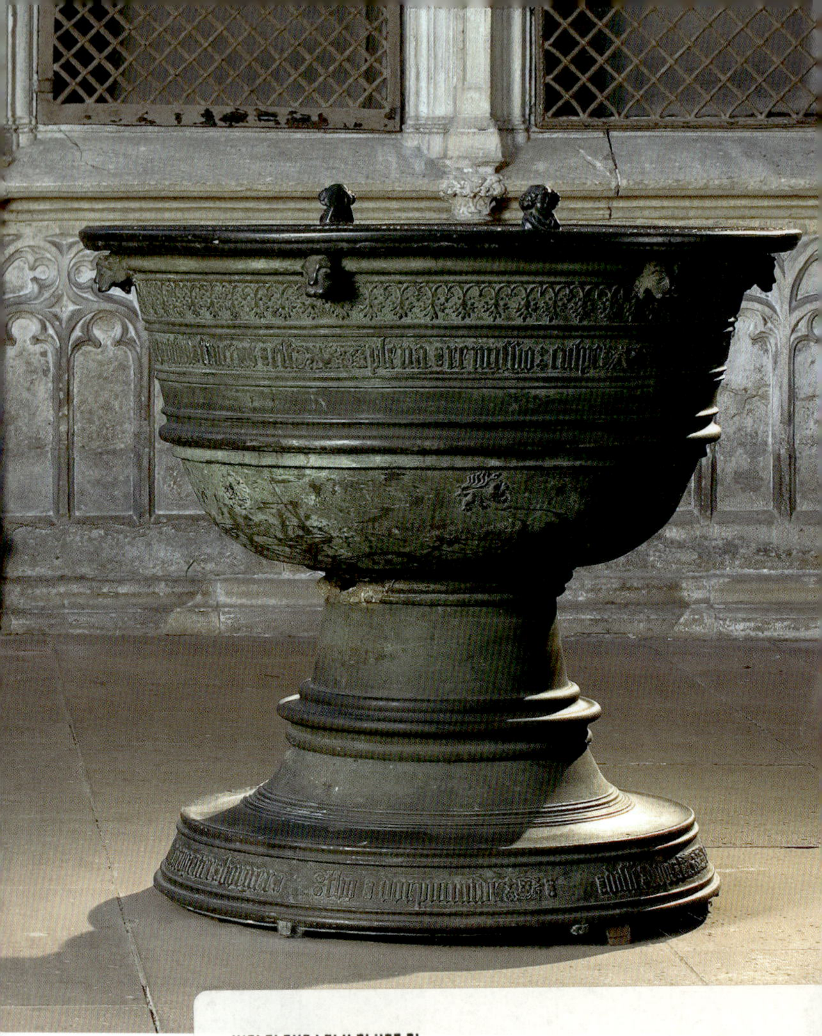

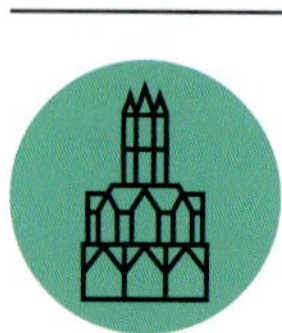

03.07.26

Schilp, T: Protestant Church St. Reinold